Snap books™

BABYSITTING

Babysitting RULES

A GUIDE FOR WHEN YOU'RE IN CHARGE

by Leah Browning

Consultant: Beth Lapp
Certified Babysitting Training Instructor

Capstone press®

Mankato, Minnesota

Snap Books are published by Capstone Press,
151 Good Counsel Drive, P.O. Box 669, Mankato, Minnesota 56002.
www.capstonepress.com

Library of Congress Cataloging-in-Publication Data

Browning, Leah.

Babysitting rules: a guide for when you're in charge / Leah Browning.

p.cm.—(Snap books. Babysitting)

Summary: "A guide for pre-teens and teens on the dos and don'ts of being a good babysitter"—Provided by publisher.

Includes bibliographical references and index.

ISBN-13: 978-0-7368-6464-0 (hardcover)

ISBN-10: 0-7368-6464-4 (hardcover)

1. Babysitting—Juvenile literature. 2. Babysitters—Conduct of life—Juvenile literature. I. Title. II. Series.

HQ769.5.L343 2007

649'.10248—dc22   2006001732

Editor: Becky Viaene

Designer: Jennifer Bergstrom

Photo Researcher/Photo Editor: Kelly Garvin

Photo Credits: Capstone Press/Karon Dubke, cover, 6–7, 9, 14–15, 17, 21, 22–23, 25; Corbis/Owaki-Kulla, 12–13; Corbis/Randy Faris, 11; Corbis/Roy Morsch, 4–5; Corbis/zefa/Grace, 8; Corbis/zefa/Roy Morsch, 19; Getty Images Inc./The Image Bank/Marc Romanelli, 26–27; Leah Browning/photo taken by Greg Becker, 32; RubberBall Productions, 28

Table of Contents

Taking Your First Steps

You've decided to become a babysitter. Congratulations! Babysitting may be one of the most entertaining, rewarding jobs you will ever have.

Before you start babysitting, there are a few rules you should know. Parents may be very different, but they all have one thing in common. They love their children and have rules they want them to follow.

When parents leave you in charge, they place a lot of trust in you. That includes trusting you to know what you should or shouldn't do while you're babysitting. After reading this book, you will understand what parents expect. Acting with respect and responsibility will help you turn into the best babysitter you can be.

Following the Rules

Every family has its own rules about how they want things to be done.

Since each family is so different, make sure that you ask about the household rules. Write down important information.

Sometimes it seems like parents have too many rules. You may not always feel like following them. However, when you are watching someone else's child, following the rules is part of your job. Even rules that don't make sense to you probably exist for a reason. Pay attention to the parents' rules about their child's bedtime, food, entertainment, language, and misbehavior.

Bedtime

A child may beg to stay up an hour later than usual "just this once." No matter how tired children are, they may refuse to sleep. Make sure you know the rules and routines for bedtime. Ask parents questions like: What time does your child go to bed? Does she have a favorite stuffed animal or blanket? Try to keep the routine as normal as possible to help the child feel more comfortable.

Food

It is important to respect parents' rules about food. Find out when and what you should feed the children. Make sure to ask if the children have allergic reactions to any foods. Don't let kids have soda or chocolate before bed. Sugary snacks can get children hyper, making it difficult for them to fall asleep.

Entertainment

Children may want to watch television, play video games, or play on the computer. Make sure you know the rules about these entertainment items. Ask parents questions like: Can they use these items? For how long? Are certain ratings forbidden? While you're babysitting, respect the parents' rules regarding what you listen to or watch also.

Helpful Hint

If you get hungry, most parents won't mind if you have a small snack. Just don't eat an entire batch of brownies or drink the last glass of milk.

Language & Misbehavior

You hope that while babysitting you'll never hear children use bad words or see them misbehave. But you need to be prepared because it could happen. Before parents leave, make sure you know what language is acceptable. Avoid using forbidden words yourself. You don't want to teach a child bad words.

Also, talk to parents about how you should handle misbehavior. Know what to do if a child says a bad word or jumps on the furniture. Some parents will deal with misbehavior when they return. Others may suggest a time out. *Never* shake, hurt, or threaten a child, no matter how frustrated you are. If the children are out of control, get help.

WHAT WOULD YOU DO?

A child's parents told you that everyone should eat only in the kitchen. The child says that his parents let him eat raisins in the living room. When you say no, he has a loud tantrum.

SIMPLE SOLUTION

Depending on how the parents want you to handle misbehavior, you may ignore the tantrum. Or you may give the child a time out. But don't give in.

You might want to be the "fun babysitter" who lets kids watch TV all night. But if parents catch you breaking the rules, they won't ask you to come back. They also won't recommend you to anyone else.

When you agree to babysit, it's important to pay attention to the parents' rules. Enforce the rules pleasantly but firmly.

Staying Safe

When you babysit, one of your biggest responsibilities is keeping the children, and yourself, safe.

Don't answer the door for anyone while you're babysitting. Delivery people can leave packages at the door or come back another time. Even the family's relatives will understand your decision to put the child's safety first and not open the door.

If you answer the phone while babysitting, don't tell callers that you're a babysitter home alone with the children. Also, don't give out private information about yourself or the family.

WHAT WOULD YOU DO?

A stranger knocks on the door. He tells you that he is the child's uncle, and that the child's parents are expecting him. You say that you can't open the door for strangers. He says, "I really need to use the bathroom. Please open the door. It's an emergency!"

SIMPLE SOLUTION

Keep the children and yourself safe. Don't open the door. Even if the man really is the child's uncle, that doesn't make it safe to let him in. The parents likely would have told you if they expected company to stop by.

Rules for Safely Handling Accidents

Although you follow the rules, accidents still may happen. Following simple rules, such as staying calm and calling for help, will allow you to handle an accident. Most accidents that may happen while you're babysitting will not be serious.

Depending on the situation, you will have to decide which number to call. If the accident is a small burn, cut, scrape, or something that isn't life-threatening, don't call 911. Instead, call the child's parents, your own parents, or a responsible adult. If a child is severely injured, unconscious, or having trouble breathing, call 911 immediately.

Emergency Phone Numbers

Cell Phone: 555-1289
Restaurant: 555-8872
Neighbor: 555-7823
Grandma: 555-7652
Fire Department: 911
Police Department: 911
Poison Control: 800-223-4567
Doctor: 555-8810

Other Times to Call Parents for Help

* A child begins to seem sick
* You become sick
* A child is hurt (more than a minor bump or scrape)
* A baby or child has been crying for 20 to 30 minutes and you can't figure out why
* The children are out of control, and you can't handle the situation

Being Respectful

How would you feel if you came home to find that someone had looked through your diary? You would probably feel angry that someone invaded your privacy.

Similarly you need to respect the privacy of the family you are babysitting for. Sometimes you need to look through the cabinets to find a clean towel or a spoon. Those things are fine. But don't search in personal drawers, read mail, or look at anything that seems private.

Barry Allen
123 Main
Centre

You should also show respect for families you babysit for by being reliable. You may want to go to a school dance, but you already agreed to babysit on the same night. The child's family is counting on you. Don't disappoint the family by canceling a babysitting job to do something else. If you must cancel a babysitting job because you are hurt or sick, call to tell the child's parents as soon as possible.

Helpful Hint

Don't do anything while the parents are gone that you wouldn't be comfortable doing right in front of them.

CHAPTER 5

Making Yourself at Home

If you babysit often, especially for the same family, you might start to feel very comfortable in their home.

But remember that it isn't actually your home. Always follow the house rules. At your house, it may be okay to watch scary movies. But when you're babysitting, watching scary movies may not be allowed.

At your house, you might leave dirty dishes on the table and throw your clothes on the floor. When you're babysitting, you need to tidy up after yourself and the children.

This does not mean that you need to vacuum the floors or scrub the toilets. But you should rinse and stack dirty dishes in the sink. Help the children pick up their toys. Picking up helps prevent injuries from tripping on toys. And the children's parents will appreciate coming home and finding everything in order.

No Friends Allowed

You might want to invite a friend over while you're babysitting. But you should never invite a friend over without asking the children's parents for permission. If you have a friend over without asking, you probably won't be asked to babysit again.

Since you shouldn't invite friends over while you're babysitting, you may want to call them. But the children could get hurt if you're on the phone, not paying attention. Remember, parents hire you to take care of their children, so skip the phone calls and visitors.

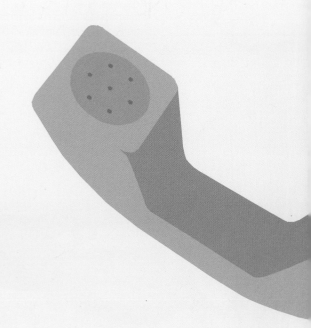

CHAPTER 6

Keeping Your Eyes Open

It's late and you feel tired. You wish you could just close your eyes and sleep for a few minutes.

Even if the children are asleep, you need to stay awake until their parents come home. It is important to make sure the children are safe. A sleeping child could wake up and be scared or need help.

Check on sleeping babies and young children every 20 to 30 minutes. Stay in a nearby room so you can hear if a child is crying or having trouble breathing.

When the children are asleep, set some rules for yourself to keep you feeling safe. Every little noise can stir up your imagination. Turn on the lights and distract yourself by reading a book or turning on some quiet music. If you want to watch TV, skip the horror movie and watch your favorite comedy instead.

Speaking Up

You agreed to babysit two children. But you find four children when you arrive to begin babysitting.

Or the parents told you that they'd be home by 10, but they don't arrive until midnight. Maybe one parent keeps underpaying you. It's time to speak up.

Sometimes parents simply made a mistake, or maybe you had a misunderstanding. Sit down with them. Calmly explain what happened and try to find a solution. Next time the parents ask you to babysit, set rules. Discuss how many children you will watch and how late you can stay before accepting the job.

Helpful Hint

If the children's parents aren't home on time, call your parents and let them know you'll be late.

A Safe Ride

Another rule you should follow is making sure you always have a safe ride home. Have a backup plan, like having your parents pick you up. Never get in the car with someone who has been drinking or is acting strange.

Helpful Hint

You may have a problem that you don't know how to handle. Ask your parents or a trustworthy adult.

Rules Rock!

Don't worry. Just because parents are counting on you to follow the rules doesn't mean you can't have fun. Babysitting is a big responsibility, but usually you can relax and just enjoy playing with the children. Rules help everyone have a safe and fun time. If you follow the rules, you'll likely be asked back to babysit over and over again.

Checklist:

Rules to Remember

- ✓ In a serious emergency, dial 911.

- ✓ *Never* shake, hurt, or threaten a child.

- ✓ Write down important instructions before the children's parents leave.

- ✓ Ask what the children are allowed to eat and drink.

- ✓ Find out which movies, TV shows, or video games are allowed.

- ✓ Take note of bedtimes and routines.

- ✓ Don't look inside drawers or explore anything that might be private.

- ✓ Tidy up after yourself and the children.

- ✓ Don't invite friends over or talk on the phone.

- ✓ Stay awake after the children go to sleep.

Glossary

allergic reaction (a-LUR-jik ree-AK-shun)—an unpleasant reaction such as a rash, breathing problems, or sneezing, caused by an allergy to something like food or pollen

private (PRYE-vit)—belonging to or concerning one person or group and no one else; private information is not meant to be shared.

solution (suh-LOO-shuhn)—the answer to a problem

unconscious (un-KON-shus)—not awake or aware of what is happening, possibly because of an illness or accident

Quick Tips

* Responsible babysitters always ask if there is something that they don't know. You might worry that asking will make you look inexperienced, but the opposite is true.

* If you have strict instructions to feed the child only certain foods, make sure that you don't offer anything else. Children may have allergies.

* Remember to tidy up, but make sure you are always watching the children. Taking care of the children is your first priority.

Read More

Brown, Harriet. *The Babysitter's Handbook: The Care and Keeping of Kids.* Middleton, Wis.: Pleasant Company, 1999.

Greene, Caroline. *The Babysitter's Handbook.* New York: DK, 1995.

Kuch, K.D. *The Babysitter's Handbook.* KidBacks. New York: Random House, 1997.

Weintraub, Aileen. *Everything You Need to Know about Being a Baby-sitter: A Teen's Guide to Responsible Child Care.* The Need to Know Library. New York: Rosen, 2000.

Internet Sites

FactHound offers a safe, fun way to find Internet sites related to this book. All of the sites on FactHound have been researched by our staff.

Here's how:

1. Visit *www.facthound.com*

2. Choose your grade level.

3. Type in this book ID **0736864644** for age-appropriate sites. You may also browse subjects by clicking on letters, or by clicking on pictures and words.

4. Click on the **Fetch It** button.

Facthound will fetch the best sites for you!

About the Author

Leah Browning has always loved babies and children. In fact, as a child, she wanted to have 12 children of her own. She grew up in New Mexico, where she began babysitting at the age of 12.

Now an adult, Leah is a stay-at-home mother and writer. Her articles, essays, stories, and poems have appeared in a variety of publications including *Mothering Magazine*, *Tucson Parent Magazine*, and *Chicken Soup for the Preteen Soul 2*.

Index